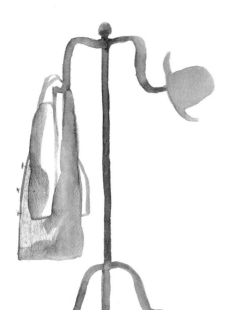

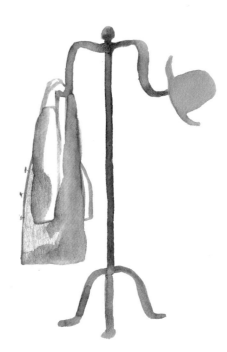

Munia
and the Day
Things Went Wrong

CAMBRIDGE UNIVERSITY PRESS
Cambridge
New York   New Rochelle
Melbourne   Sydney

Munia was fast asleep.
'Munia! It's time to get up. It's past 8 o'clock!'
called her mother.
Munia pretended not to hear and pulled the bedclothes
over her head.

After a while her mother came back.
'Munia! It's time . . .'
'Munia's not here.'
'Come on, don't be silly!'
'I'M NOT HERE! I told you . . .'
Her mother pulled the bedclothes off her.
Brrr! It was cold. Munia got up.
She was in a BAD MOOD.

'Why do I have to   go to school?' shouted Munia
at breakfast, and kicked her sister, Andrea,
under the table.
'I think you've got out of bed the wrong
side today, Munia,' said her mother.
'All right,' thought Munia, 'if they think
I'm bad, then I'm going to be VERY BAD.'

Her father took her to school.
'Goodbye Munia, cheer up!' he said.
Munia didn't even say goodbye.

At school things went from bad to worse.
First she spilled some red poster paint.
'Oh Munia!' said the teacher.
Then she tore up her friend Maria's picture.
'Oh dear, Munia!' said the teacher. 'What IS wrong
with you today?'
Then she had a fight with Tony, because he'd borrowed
her pencil.
'Munia! Munia!' said the teacher. 'Just calm down.
And say you're sorry.'
But Munia wouldn't.
When it was singing, she wouldn't sing, and when it
was playtime she wouldn't play.

At last it was time to go home.
But Munia didn't want to go.
She saw Tony's grandfather, who had come to fetch Tony.
'Hallo!' said Munia. 'Tony's Mama said I could come
home to tea with him.'

'Nobody ever tells me anything!' grumbled Tony's grandfather.
'All right, come along with us.'
Tony lived in an old house right in the middle of the village.
'Why didn't you tell me you'd invited Munia to tea?'
said grandfather to Tony's mother.
'Nobody ever tells me anything,' he added, grumbling.

'But I haven't invited her to tea!' said Tony's mother.
'Well she said you had, and she's here!'
'I'll telephone the school right away. Her father will
be looking for her.'
She was right. Munia's father had been looking all over
the place. First he'd looked in the playground. No Munia.
Then he'd looked in all the classrooms. Still no Munia.
Where was she?
Munia was at Tony's house. She and Tony were sliding
down the banisters. It was quite fun. But then Munia
slid down so fast that she couldn't stop.
WHAM! She hit the wooden post and it BROKE!
Just at that moment, Munia's father walked in.
'Oh Munia! What HAVE you DONE?'

When Munia and her father got home, the rest of the
family were already having tea.
'Well, Munia, what sort of a day did you have?' asked
her mother.
But Munia wouldn't say anything.
Straight after tea, she ran out of the house and down
the lane. She came to a gate with cows on the other side.
They watched her with their sad velvety eyes.
'Their eyelashes are like soft brushes,' thought Munia
and climbed on to the gate to have a closer look at them.
She knew she was going to do something VERY BAD INDEED.
She couldn't stop herself.
She opened the gate and out came the cows. First one,
rather slowly, and then the rest of them. Nobody
stopped them and so they walked on down the lane until
they came to Munia's house. Munia had left the gate open.
The first cow stopped and looked in. Then she walked in
through the open gate. The other cows trooped after her.
In no time at all the flowerbeds were trampled, the flowers
were eaten and there were cowpats all over the grass.

'Hey! What's happening!' Munia's father rushed out of
the house and started to shoo the cows out of the garden.
The poor cows were frightened and didn't know where to go.
Then Munia's mother and Andrea came out of the house.
'Munia! Come and help us!'
But Munia wouldn't.
At last they drove the cows out of the garden, back up
the lane, through the gate, and into the field again.
'Munia, this is really too much,' said her mother.
'Go to your room,' said her father.

Munia lay on her bed and looked out of
the window. She lay there for a long time.
Suddenly she sniffed the air. What was
that lovely smell? Hot chocolate!

Then she heard Andrea laugh.
'What if they don't love me any more?' thought Munia.
Suddenly she didn't want to be bad any more.
'What if they don't want me any more?' she thought.
'What if they won't forgive me for being bad?'

Munia crept downstairs. She saw her mother's old jacket hanging in the hall and her old blue hat. She put them on and crept out of the house by the front door. She walked all the way round the house, through the garden and knocked at the back door.

Her mother opened the door.
'Hallo! she said, surprised.
'Good afternoon, I am Mrs Blinco and I have come to call
on you.'

'Ah, Mrs Blinco! Do come in. We were just going to have
something to eat. You'll stay and have a cup of hot
chocolate with us, I hope?'
'If it's no trouble . . .' answered Mrs Blinco very politely.
'Of course not! Come in and sit down.'
Mrs Blinco went into the kitchen and said 'Good afternoon'
very seriously to her father and sister. She sat down at
the kitchen table and her mother put a large cup of hot
chocolate in front of her. Her father hid his face behind
his napkin.
'What's he laughing at?' asked Mrs Blinco.
'Don't take any notice of him. He's like that sometimes,'
answered Munia's mother. 'Let me give you a little more
hot chocolate.'

'Don't you have a daughter called Munia?' asked Mrs Blinco.
'Yes, we *had*,' answered Munia's father.
'You mean she's not here any more?' Mrs Blinco looked worried.
'Well, you see,' explained her mother, 'Munia doesn't
seem very happy at home. Today she's been so VERY BAD
that we think perhaps she wants a different family.
Perhaps she doesn't love us any more.'
'But . . . do you still love her? Or would you rather have . . .
er . . . a different daughter?'
'Oh no,' said Munia's mother. 'We still love her very
much, don't we?'
'Oh yes!' said Andrea with a laugh.
'Of course we do,' answered Munia's father.
'I think Munia loves you very much too,' said Mrs Blinco.
'The thing is sometimes everything goes wrong and
she just wants to be BAD.'
'Do you think this is going to happen very often?'
asked Munia's mother, sounding worried.
'Munia doesn't want it to happen, I'm sure,' said
Mrs Blinco.
'Oh no, of course not!' said everybody.
Mrs Blinco stood up and said, 'Well, thank you very much
for the lovely hot chocolate. I hope that girl Munia is
not going to be bad any more.'
'Goodbye Mrs Blinco. Come back whenever you like . . .'
'Goodbye and thank you!' and Mrs Blinco disappeared
into the garden.

After a little while there was
another knock at the door.
Munia's mother opened it again.
'I've come back, Mama!'
It was Munia, and she had
a little smile on her face.'

The End

I'd like to introduce myself. My name is Asun Balzola. I've always loved drawing, ever since I was very small. When I was at school I used to doodle all over my books. Some of my teachers got very cross. (Others couldn't stop laughing!) When I grew up I started writing and drawing for children. I'm very lucky, I've won a lot of prizes in Spain and other countries and I've travelled to exhibitions all over the world with my books. I love my work. I also love the sea, the countryside, ice-creams in summer, animals, coloured pencils and lots of other things. I hope you will enjoy my books about Munia.

Published by the Press Syndicate of the University of Cambridge
The Pitt Building, Trumpington Street, Cambridge CB2 1RP
32 East 57th Street, New York, NY 10022, USA
10 Stamford Road, Oakleigh, Melbourne 3166, Australia

Originally published in Spanish as
Munia y la Señora Piltronera
© Asun Balzola
© Ediciones Destino, S.A., Barcelona 1984

First published in English by the Cambridge University Press 1988 as
Munia and the Day Things Went Wrong.
English adaptation © Cambridge University Press 1988

Printed in Spain

British Library cataloguing in publication data
Balzola, Azun
Munia and the day things went wrong.
I. Title II. Munia y la Señora Piltronera.
English
863′.64[J]

Library of Congress cataloguing-in-publication data
Balzola, Asun.
Munia and the day things went wrong.
Translation of: Munia y la Señora Piltronera.
Summary: When Munia wakes up in a bad mood and sees
her well-behaved sister, she decides to spend the day
being wicked.
[1. Behaviour–Fiction. 2. Family life–Fiction]
I. Title
PZ7.B2148Mn   1988   [E]   87–35797
ISBN 0-521-35643-1
D. L. B-1.352-88